REMEMBRANCE

OF

THINGS

PRESENT

(A Trilogy)

- James H. Kurt -

AuthorHouse™
1663 Liberty Drive
Bloomington, IN 47403
www.authorhouse.com
Phone: 1 (800) 839-8640

Nihil Obstat:
Rev. Msgr. Robert F. Coleman, J.C.D.
Censor Librorum
September 13, 2017

Imprimatur:
+ Cardinal Joseph W. Tobin, C.Ss.R.
Archbishop of Newark, New Jersey
October 4, 2017

The Nihil Obstat and Imprimatur are official declarations that a book or pamphlet is free of doctrinal error. No implication is contained therein that those who have granted the Nihil Obstat and Imprimatur agree with the contents, opinions, or statements expressed.

Scripture taken from the Revised Standard Version: Catholic Edition, copyright 1965, 1966, Division of Christian Education of the National Council of the Churches of Christ in the United States of America. Used by permission. All rights reserved.

Published by AuthorHouse 12/11/2017

ISBN: 978-1-5462-1335-2 (sc)
ISBN: 978-1-5462-1334-5 (e)

Print information available on the last page.

All artwork and design by James Kurt.

This book is printed on acid-free paper.

"In God's hand is the life of every living thing
and the breath of all mankind."

Job 12:10

THE QUESTION

How to get to the present moment…
and record it?
Or is it impossible?

Something is dancing round in my brain…
there is light, somewhere.
But who can trace it, who can find it?
Who can uncover what is always here?

Can it be done only in things that are past,
even if only recently, even if only today…?
Or would the LORD allow a glimpse of His presence
to be revealed?

Here we have the question.
(The answer I don't yet know.)

St. John, pray for us!

Table of Contents

Preface

To write of the present seems impossible.

To touch the present moment one must first remember the LORD's NAME (YHWH), for it is our means to the LORD, Who it is lives in the present moment.

Then one must remember the presence of Christ within us in the Sacrament we receive – He is really with us, in the present moment.

Then perhaps the Spirit might inspire us to write in remembrance of things present. But it seems this would have to be in vision of Heaven (which is why I was moved to invoke St. John's intercession).

For only God and the things of God exist in the present, and so one would have to step into the realm of God to speak of things present.

One could *live* in the present by remembering God's NAME and His presence in us in the Sacrament, and by the Spirit's power; but how can one *write* of things present, for it would seem they would immediately be past, or have to be future...? (Is it not only silence that is present?)

Will the LORD have to take me through the curtain of time?

1

SILENCE

"It is better to remain silent and to be
than to talk and not be...
He who has the Word of Jesus
can also listen to His Silence."

St. Ignatius of Antioch
(Office of Readings, OT 2 Mon.)

God speaks in silence; and so, in the present moment, where God exists, there is only silence – there are no words. And so how can words speak of the present? They cannot. Unless they are blessed by the LORD with His silence.

One knows the silence of the LORD, the silence of the present moment (where there are no words) especially in adoration of the Blessed Sacrament. Here the silence speaks so clearly; here it radiates like light. The Sacrament is silent, but this silence speaks to our hearts.

I am present now before the Blessed Sacrament exposed upon the altar...

Let me approach you, LORD.

The Center of My Skull

There is a silence at the center of our skulls that is like the silence of the LORD (we are made in His image after all), and there He speaks His NAME to us: "YHWH". There the Spirit fans the flame of our mind, which is like His own (we are made in His image after all), and a light shines. And we have nothing left to say. For we have entered His presence and there is no need for words.

Speak, LORD, your servant is listening.

The Crucifix

There is a large crucifix on the wall behind the altar,
and here, too, the silence speaks;
for Jesus has no words for us now,
so we must listen to His silence.

And this silence cries out to our hearts,
cries out of His love for us…
    and His heart begins to beat in our own
    (we are made in His image after all) –
    to this beating He calls us to listen,
    and respond in kind.

Let it be so, O LORD!

The Candle

The candle flickers. Do you see it?
Do you hear it speak?
It speaks of the silence of our LORD
    and shines with His fire.

Here, too, is silence.
Here, too, we approach the LORD
    in the present moment.

O Spirit of God, breathe through my mind
    and set my soul aflame with your love,
    that I may see,
    that I may hear YHWH's voice
        speaking to my heart…

and that I may write according to His will.

Sea of Glass

There is a sea of glass mingled with fire, the fire of the
LORD, the fire of the Spirit burning brightly, illumining all it
touches. As if between mountains it stands, and flows on
endlessly, to the ends of Heaven and earth.

How smooth is the sea, and how transparent: all can be seen
in these waters. Like the bush burning but not consumed, like
the Blessed Virgin from whom comes new life, the life of the

world, this sea is life-giving. And the more it gives of its graces, the greater they become.

All around the sea of glass, the angels stand with trumpets in their hands, and the saints bow down to the LORD who sits upon His throne above the sea of glass. The Heavens open and light pours forth, with a peace that transcends understanding. And so, all are silent.

Even in their singing, all are silent, for all are filled with the presence of God, His NAME written upon their hearts and glorified by their souls that sing forever of His power, of His unending power founded in His everlasting love.

O what love is here! For O how our God is present, present in all things – and so all things sing of His glory and love.

O let us be surrounded by your Presence, LORD! O let us live in your light! Let us be immersed in your love and mercy and so stand forever in your sight. May we dwell upon the sea of glass with you and drink of its fruits.

The Light in Our Minds

The light in our minds is the fire of the Holy Spirit; like a candle it burns at the center of our skulls, fanned by the Breath of the LORD upon our face... In the beginning the LORD breathed into our nostrils the breath of life, and we became a living soul. And still we are living souls breathing His Spirit, those who are in a state of grace, remaining close to our God.

And He speaks to us, speaks to our souls, calling us to listen to the lamp He lights in our minds. His simple creatures we must be, walking as if through a Garden in the evening with Him.

O what blessed conversation is here, here in His presence! (I sit again – and always – before the Blessed Sacrament exposed on the altar.) Here it is easy to feel His Breath upon us, His light shining in our minds... Here it is easy to be His simple creatures.

The crown of His Creation man is made in the sight of God, and this crown we rediscover by the grace of Our Lord Jesus Christ. He restores us to our place at the feet of the Father, making us His children once more.

O let us be remade in the image of Jesus, the only Son of the living God. Then light shall shine in our minds; then we shall breathe as one with the Holy Spirit.

The Voice

There is a voice that speaks above the din (in a pronounced Silence) and it calls all hearts to their home in the light of Heaven. It calls us now to stop where we are and listen to that voice, else we shall remain deaf all our lives, all our actions performed in vain.

The voice calls clearly (in silence) and is present everywhere, if only we would care to listen, if only our hearts were open to such a simple and loving call. It is a voice that none could miss, if they would stop speaking (even for a moment).

But who is open to such a call; who can hear it at all... and who even cares that it is there, always calling out in love? How happy we seem to be to rush through our lives with barely a thought for where we are going.

But the voice does not stop calling; it is ever present, and ever shall be. God does not stop loving us and He cannot go away… however much we ignore Him.

When the light comes down from on high, we will be able to ignore Him no more: His voice will be all that is heard. (O how wonderful it will be!) It would be wise to listen now, to seek indeed the love and wisdom to which that voice leads, if we care at all for our souls.

Speak, LORD, your servant is listening, though often he may be distracted.

Breathe

Breathe in the moment, be in the moment… be in His presence. Do not be afraid to use your senses; they are not your enemy but a window unto eternity. See the things that are present all around you – they can be a means to the LORD.

The air conditioner rumbles lightly in the background; light pours through two large stained glass windows either side of the altar (and through a skylight). There is also electric light. The large crucifix is there on the wall behind the altar, the tabernacle directly underneath… and Jesus is exposed in the monstrance (as always). The candles flicker either side.

I sit on the tile floor before the first pew. The chapel is large, able to seat more than a hundred easily. This is the scene. It is perhaps more detail than is needed to begin to breathe, to begin to become aware of the presence of the LORD, but the naming of things can help.

I remember once I tapped into the Spirit breathing in our midst, and intimately the NAME of God and His presence became known to me. I was walking alone in the evening, naming things... The experience is recorded in the lyrics of "WH": "Autumn Leaves Swirl About My Feet, / Lightly Along The Way / In The Park. // ... Trees. Grass. Path. / Fence. Road. Car. // ... Light. Wind. / God. Father. / WH?" And there I was. And there He was. Breathing in me. In the silence.

No words. No thoughts. Nothing other than the awareness of His presence, His being there with me.

And all I could do was breathe.

Silence in the City

O LORD, should I stay here in my place before your altar, before your presence singing out for all to hear... here where you are so near? Or should I go out into the city and there discover and speak of your divine silence present even amidst the noise, the distractions of the world?

This is what I did with *silence in the city*; I realize now that this book was indeed a remembrance of things present, a capturing of moments of contemplation, of your holy presence – of the speaking of your holy NAME – outside (and sometimes inside) the doors of the church. So, what I seek to do it seems I have already done... or do you call me to more?

I do not know if I should stay and write only here where the silence is so palpable, where you are so present, or take my pen and notebook into the world. Please guide me as you have so faithfully done in this journey to you and my seeking of your will.

If I stay here, of what shall I speak? It would seem you would have to provide visions; for what my eyes can see in this place is limited, but your vision is not limited by anything.

And so I pray, let your vision come to my eyes – I give them to you along with my heart, my soul... all my life. Let your will be done.

Praise you, LORD, my God!

Carry Me Away

Carry me away, LORD, in your arms.
Carry me far from this place
    to the place where you rest.
Surround me with your cloud of peace
and envelop me in your light...
Carry me away, LORD, in your arms,
    in your love this day, this night.

All we see is darkness when we look
    toward you, O LORD.
Our eyes are not able to see you
    on your throne in the Kingdom.
You are surrounded as by a cloud,
    keeping us from entering.

But you reach down
    and take us in your loving arms
    and carry us through the darkness
    to your very heart.

And you hold us close to you
    so we can hear your heart beat
    for us,
    so we can know your love.

And so, you are very close indeed,
    closer than we are to ourselves.
Though there seems to be no way to you,
    we are already there.

Beating Heart

Wrapped as though in gauze in the womb of our mother, all we hear is the beat of a heart, your heart, and all we know is your presence surrounding us in this place. This is our home, our place of rest in this world, and here is perfect peace. Nothing can touch us or enter to harm us in this sanctuary.

O what joy it brings to listen to your heartbeat, to know your presence with us. Our bodies are like stone balloons, so heavy and so light, even at the same time – like the Cross itself. Jesus has come to dwell among us, and so in our presence your heart does beat… carrying us away.

What can I say?

Here in this sanctuary there are no words, no need for them at all, for all is spoken by you in the beat of this heart. What is there but love?

And so we but swim along in your all-encompassing love, carried to your Kingdom.

Your Face

Show your face to me, LORD, and that will be enough. This is what we ask here in the dark as we long for Him. We are like Moses, with whom the LORD shared His NAME and thus revealed to him His back. We, too, wish to see His face.

But His face has been revealed to us. Moses spoke with Him face to face and still could not see Him, but we to whom Jesus has come should not be blind as Philip. The apostles walked and talked with Him and looked upon His visage, yet they did not understand that the LORD was in their presence – for He and the Father are one: He is the Father's Image.

When I kneel before you, Lord, close to the monstrance, I see your face in that white Host and am aware of your presence. But still there is a glass between us that seems to keep you hidden. Is it not the darkness of my eyes that causes them to fall short of vision of your presence?

There is yet greater glory that awaits us when you return and all is fulfilled... but here in the silence before your altar is all we need to see. Here indeed your face is revealed.

Ash Wednesday

Let the writer quit his pen before the altar and sit in silent adoration of the LORD's presence. Why should he speak here where even the angels are quiet? Let all the earth bow down before Him, abandoning their occupations.

Listen. Let us rather listen than speak, and let His light fill us. Let us call out for such blessing from deep within our souls.

Let the parade cease – why should we be so busy? There is nothing that matters but the LORD and His wisdom.

Put down your pen, James. Why do you keep writing? You cannot speak of my majesty or capture the glory of my presence. Your words will mean nothing in the end... though now I grant them a measure of light.

I will be silent, O LORD. Let me be silent here in your presence, before your throne. Let me know nothing but being with you.

Let me repent of all my words, of all my useless actions, and glorify you with my presence, with an ear and a heart open to your Word.

Thank you for your Silence.

No Words

How can I speak no words?

How can I make the NAME of God known?

How can I enter His presence with my writing?

There are no words where the LORD dwells; in His House there is but silence. But the words on this page make a sound – they are meant to be spoken, to be read.

Still, there is a way. There is a silence in the words themselves, both on the page and in the air. For by the grace of the LORD, He speaks through them.

Just as He has given us His NAME – YHWH – through His prophet Moses; just as He has thus made pronounceable that which is beyond words... so He can speak in and through all words. His silence He can make known.

He has made it known for our sakes, that we might approach Him where He Is. He does not wish us to remain apart from His presence, but sharing in His glory for eternity. This is His will.

And His will is done on earth as it is in Heaven. His Son has come to walk among us and His silence is present all around us... and within us. (In fact, we cannot escape it.)

And so, though these are but words on a page, though we are but frail human souls, He breathes His life, His presence, His silence, into both our souls and the words; and so we speak of His Silence.

Swimming in Silence

O let us swim in the silence, rising and falling with the beat of Christ's heart. It will be better than swimming with dolphins, for to this dance there is no end. And no beginning. Once we enter into God's presence, we are grafted to His eternal Tree.

To dwell in eternity, to enter His heart... to swim in joy on the tide of the waters that flow from Jesus' side – this is our desire.

And this is what we find here before His Presence on the altar; this comes to us now in His light. His light fills our minds with a sense of His glory, His eternal glory, where we hope to swim forever.

We rise and fall with the beat of Christ's heart; His blood washes over us, renewing our souls and opening our eyes to the glory that awaits in His Silence.

Let us spin in circles, let us dance for joy through our tears – these, too, wash us clean and enable us to see... He is coming, soon. His Kingdom is upon us.

I am not worthy to be called your son, O LORD, but you reach down and lift me up and cradle me to your heart, where I may swim in silence.

Pierced Heart

Here in your presence my heart is pierced as your own, as that of your Mother; you share with me the blood of your Cross. It is as though a sword enters my throat and all I can do is prophesy in your Name of your glory, the glory that comes by way of the Cross.

How sweet is this pierced heart, this union with you in your sacrifice for our sakes. How sweet you are to share with me this blessing, to think of me and offer me a drop of your own blood, a measure of your sweet pain.

O LORD, what glory is here in the blood of your Son, in the sacrifice He has made for our sins. Indeed, how sweet are the nails that hold Him there upon the Tree of our salvation. O that all men were prophets, that all could share in the blessing of your Cross and declare its glory to all!

Jesus, let me embrace your feet, your wounds, and the blood that comes from them. Let me taste of your love and know that blood flowing through my veins.

This pierced heart is all I desire, for in it, all I desire is fulfilled. O Lord, let my heart beat with your own!

Nail Marks

O Lord, I seem to feel your nail marks in my hands, in the palms of my hands. This is a great gift you share with me – may it never leave; may it become more real.

I do not often find them there, but here before you it comes back to me this day… Let me bleed with you. I feel as if I am at the foot of the Cross; and is there a better place to be on this earth? Here where the most blessed among us, your Mother and John (and Mary Magdalene), were privileged to stand; here, too, we all find the grace that pours forth from your hands.

O Lord, I am so close to you now, so physically near your presence in the Sacrament... please let me be as close spiritually – let my prayers, my life, not be in vain.

It is when I am alive with you, as I am now, that I feel your nail marks in my hands. Let me be alive with you wherever I am, that I shall not forget you and the sacrifice you have made; that I shall not forget it is by your blood I am saved. Let me cherish your nail marks in my hands.

Transport Me

Transport me, LORD, from this place to where you are. When I am with you, I will no longer need to be concerned with any pain that comes from sitting on these tiles; this pain will be no more. But only you can take me where you are, and only by your grace.

You dwell now in perfect light, in perfect peace (in Silence). You are present even at this moment in your holy Kingdom with your angels and your saints... How shall I come there and join in their number? How shall I come to where you are?

I seem to hear the angels singing and the saints praising your holy NAME; my eyes seem almost ready to look upon the light of your face – but I am not in vision. I am just sitting here before you again on this hard tile floor, and writing in this book. What can I do, O LORD?

If you would come to carry me away, I would go with you, LORD; but perhaps I would die at such grace and wonder come upon me. But inside, at least... reach down inside of me and take my breath and the beat of my heart – raise at least these up to your presence, to the place where you dwell, now and forever.

His Bowed Head

The arch of Heaven opens up above the bowed head of our Savior upon the Cross. He has died but new life has come to all Creation.

Here we dwell under the dome of clouds, the sky set between the clouds and the sea, between the waters above and the waters below... Here is where we live and breathe, the home God made for us.

But the sacrifice of Christ pierces the heavens and brings us to His Kingdom, a place beyond the clouds and sea (which will be rolled up and disappear on the last Day).

How blessed is our Savior's head as it bows upon the Cross for our sakes, as He fulfills the will of the Father and gives up His Spirit. This bowed head is truly beautiful. The day may be the darkest of all days, but His willing sacrifice makes it eternally bright.

It opens the gates of Heaven for us, tearing the curtain in two and allowing all souls who join themselves to it to enter the Holy of Holies.

Let us bow our heads with Him and see the sky open above.

Inside These Walls

A bird sings outside these walls, but I do not really hear it, am not concerned about it. I'm sure its song is beautiful, especially on this dark day after the rain… but inside is something beyond beauty, beyond the pleasing song of a bird on a new morning – in this place the LORD of Heaven and earth sits upon His throne in silence. And nothing is more beautiful than this.

In these walls is contained the Body, Blood, Soul, and Divinity of our Lord Jesus Christ, and it is revealed to our eyes on this altar. Within these walls the Spirit breathes, the church like a lung of God. Inside these walls is a Paradise to which the bird's song cannot compare. This is another place, another time.

What goes on outside these walls does not matter, though I pray it shall all be blessed. But I am inside these walls now and wish only to look upon the face of Christ.

And I know that my breathing here, my being in the presence of the LORD, serves as a blessing not only to me but also to the world. The hub upon which the world spins is silent and sure, and here is the hub of the wheel, here is the Breath of God… here is that which gives light to the world, here inside these walls.

Face to Face

My LORD, I believe you spoke to Moses face to face, like one speaks to any man; and I believe you imparted your words to him and that he set these words down, conveying them to others of his time… and that they come down to us this day. I believe these are your words. And so, from Genesis to Revelation I believe it is you who speak to us, and not any man.

Why do even so many in the Church not believe? Why do they at least seem to make excuse for your words, your Word? Why have they lost all sense of prophecy?

LORD, I believe you could speak to me even now face to face and convey what you will. If Moses was able, then why not those of our own time, who have not only the revelation of your NAME but the Body and Blood of your Son and the Holy Spirit upon them? Should we not be better able to know you face to face? And yet we don't.

LORD, I believe I look upon your face here in the Sacrament on this altar. You light up my face with your Presence. Still, I cannot say I speak with you face to face. But I believe that if you willed it, it could be so. And I want you to know that I believe you could do so, and that I would accept such a call.

Let your Word be upon my soul.

Bread

Bread. There is but bread here, is there not? I see the grain... but I see here, too, the lines of your face, the image of your presence among us, before us in this Bread.

This thin wafer held between the fingers of a man, raised up to Heaven in your Name, becomes your very presence with us, Lord. How can this be? How can you come to us so humbly? And how can I see you here in this Bread?

What grace you give to us, O Lord, to come to us here, almost invisibly, in this Sacrament. And you are broken for our sakes; you make yourself so vulnerable and allow yourself to be broken, so easily, by human hands. How you love us, Lord!

And since you are Bread, you are to be eaten, chewed by human teeth – as the martyrs were chewed by the teeth of the lions, as all the food of the earth is chewed by our teeth... and so you feed us. And this Bread brings us to Heaven, for you are present there and you are present in Heaven, always. O make us one with you!

In this Bread before me I see your face; I see you looking into my eyes. May I hold that gaze wherever I go, wherever I am in this world. Feed me always with your presence, here, so really, so humbly, in our midst.

Buzzing

What of the buzzing of the electric lights overhead, the constant buzzing of modern life? What shall we make of it here where eternity rests?

Outside the stained glass windows cars race past. In the past the clanking air conditioner in a church became for me the wings of angels thundering close to my beating heart, illumining my eyes and mind... But here today, what shall we make of the constant buzzing? What can I say of it, LORD? In this, what should we hear?

How can you coexist with the noise, the mundane and distracting sounds of human life? How can you be here at all? Is it not your humility I hear today? Is it not your unconquerable vulnerability you reveal? There is nothing that can take us away from you; you are indeed everywhere, and there is nothing greater than your presence among us.

And so, let the buzzing and creaking and slamming go on; let the cars whir by on their frantic journeys... The roar of motors cannot detract from your love and glory that come to us this day in the Bread upon your altar.

I love you, LORD. Your Silence continues even amidst the noise.

All Will Be Still

All will be still one day; and the noise shall fall to silence as only Silence reigns. The motors shall cease, the buzzing stop, as all becomes subject to the LORD. Then we shall hear as we ought.

But what of now, O LORD, and what of the noise inside of me? What of the times I am in the frantic car, behind the wheel? What of the hours there is no silence in my skull?

In these times I must recognize the noise and hold to your promise that all will be still one day, that all may become still if I but turn to you, remembering your presence and how you are calling me in the moment.

Every moment you call to us; in all things you would instruct us. We can always hear your voice over the din, if we would but listen. And it always imparts wisdom.

Every situation can be turned to good; in every place the LORD's Silence speaks, for at the heart of all is His NAME. So the stillness is never far from us, again, if we would but ask and listen.

If some temptation comes, some noise not of the Kingdom, it can be a catalyst to prayer and the seeking of forgiveness. Listen to the LORD speak each day in His Word and in all the things around you. Remember always the present moment in which He ever speaks… and you will find the stillness there.

Seraphim

Like the Seraphim who gaze upon you always, so are we who kneel here in your presence and look upon the Sacrament. Here is your throne room and here you sit upon the altar exposed to our eyes, our poor mortal vision.

And how the light of your Presence stills my tongue and brings silence to the center of my skull! How in that silence I am able to sing of your glory before my face! How glorious is your Presence. Open our ears and our hearts to hear the Seraphim sing of your glory.

How can I be here, O LORD? I want to stay here forever as do the Seraphim whose faces are always turned toward you. Never let me leave. Let me hear the angels' wings echoing through your Kingdom – bring me to Heaven where you reign.

So thunderous is the sound made by angels' wings in the Silence of your Kingdom. And high above it all you sit as the holy Seraphim give you due honor and praise, as they adore you in all your glory, LORD.

Here we are blessed with a taste of that glory, and it overwhelms our minds as we are encompassed by your surpassing light.

Holy, holy, holy LORD God of power and might!

Heaven and earth are filled with your glory!

Hosanna in the highest!

Striving

Striving. I am striving, O LORD, to find your Word upon my soul despite the sickness within me. You are still there, in the stillness, in the silence, in the Blessed Sacrament… but I am so distracted. Should I be here at all?

How unchanging you are, O LORD. How you remain as you are, waiting for us to come to you. But we are so changing, so inconstant… How shall we find you? The stillness can come to us even in this sickness, for nothing could keep you from us.

Open my nostrils, LORD, that I may breathe, breathe as one with you in the clear light of day and not suffer any separation come from sickness, from my imperfections. Meet me in my striving toward you.

The sickness can help us to find you; the suffering can calm our souls even as our bodies decay. That our souls are well is all we seek, all we need… and so, bless the sickness that brings us closer to you.

O let me be healed, healed by your presence! Breathe in me this day, dear LORD, and I shall be set free from all evil as I draw close to you. Please put your arms around me, LORD, and comfort my ailing soul.

The Devil's Whisper

You are unaffected, too, by the whispering of the devil, the accusations he throws at you all the while we are here on this earth and you are with us. Even here in your House, even here before your altar, he does not cease his attack on your presence, seeking to distract even the most devout soul from being with you.

But these whispers are as nothing to you who remain unchanged before us, unmoved by their attempts at deception. How steady is your love for us! How eternal is your glory!

Give us, O LORD, your same steadfastness in the face of evil; help us, too, to remain unaffected by the devil's temptations, by the accusations he throws at us, by his whisperings. Cast from us forever the wiles of Satan.

May St. Michael thrust him into hell with all his angels, that the whispering may cease and we may rejoice in your holy presence with nothing to distract us, nothing to lead us apart from your love.

It is for this day we wait and pray. In the meantime give us strength and let us be ever at peace in your presence.

Thank you, LORD, for your light.

Guard Your Mouth

O LORD, how shall I learn to guard my mouth, to watch my tongue and all the words I speak, not to open my lips in vain? How can I keep a steady eye on that which my eye cannot see, that to which I am so blind? How shall I come to realize my words are not my own and are not to be wasted or used for ill? How shall silence become my goal, the bar by which I judge my words?

When I was sick, I couldn't speak, and this was indeed a blessing. Now I am well and my mouth is opened for all kinds of foolishness, anger and impatience. What shall save me, LORD?

I should say nothing, like a Carthusian or a Camaldolese – this is what I should realize. And so, whatever I do speak will be spoken with love, watching carefully what I say. For the words are yours, O LORD, and so I should treat them as I do all things; I should be as economical with them as with my money and goods and time, and writing. But they are wasted like water futilely flowing from a tap.

O help me to mind my words, indeed to keep careful watch over my lips – to guard my mouth. Help me to see my mouth with the eye of my mind and watch every word that comes out. Only by your grace can this be done. Only by your instruction can I learn. Please let your Silence stay with me and let it ever be my guide.

The Machines Stop Running

The machines stop running; they are silenced in your Presence – nothing made by the hand of man will stand on that Day. There will not be left one stone upon another.

Today it is the air conditioner that stops immediately as I kneel before you, LORD, and this indicates to me clearly the silence to which all the vain enterprises of man are relegated in the end, when you come again. Already all is fulfilled by you; on that Day it will be known.

Even the machine that is our body, insofar as it opposes our soul, insofar as it falls short of doing your will, will be silenced: with Job we will have to put our hands over our mouth. (There is nothing we can say in your presence.)

How the world runs on in the ways devised by man... In themselves the machines are not bad – how could they be, since they are but machines? But how they take over the lives of men! How man makes a treadmill upon which he traps himself, unable to escape his own inventions.

We must bow down before the LORD, and before Him alone. Beware of idols, my son.

Present

O LORD, you are all that is present. Nothing else has life except through you, for you are Life itself and share that Life with us only by your grace. Otherwise, we are dead. And nothing that is dead is present.

O LORD, let us come into your presence; let us be present with you. Shine your light upon us that we might be alive this day, this hour. With your angels and saints in Heaven let us dwell, for only they are truly present with you.

We have eternal life in us, we know, for you have told us so. By the grace of our Baptism, by the favor of our faith in you, your Spirit lives in us. And your Spirit is life eternal. But still we are blind, LORD; still we do not find ourselves present to you.

But we do have faith, and that faith draws us close to you, close to your presence (as I am so close before you this day). We feel your heart beat within us keeping the time of Heaven, and we sense your light upon us illumining our minds... and we know we are with you. O let us draw closer to your presence!

We long for the day when we shall enter into your joy and sing with the angels your praise. Open our mouths this day to praise you, and your presence will not be far away.

"My Jesus!"

I cry to you, my Savior, for your grace and secure protection on this day, in this place... Surround me with your presence.

Because you are here I know that God saves, for you are His salvation: Y'shua (YHWH saves). His Silence becomes a cleansing shower pouring upon us from Heaven. The Father is made known in the salvation you bring to the world in your blood shed on the Cross.

O my Jesus! How I love you, or I should say: How you love us! For it is your love that comes to us and inflames our hearts with that same love, bringing us alive in the presence of God. And the Father is with us. And we are His sons – through you we become His children.

O Jesus, how you enliven our souls; how you illumine our minds and make our hearts beat – truly, life is found in you alone. You are the only Way to eternal life, to the Father in Heaven.

There let us dwell with you, Lord; let us never be separated from your saving grace, from the light of your face... Forever let us sing your praise! And forever we shall be with you, even as you are with us now.

How wonderful is your presence, LORD.

The Way In

Yesterday it was by acknowledging the things surrounding – that which I could see, hear, and feel – that I was led to see you, Lord, and exclaim your Name. Then I tried to do the same afterward in a supermarket parking lot (naming the things surrounding, what I could sense), and by this means was again led to your presence, which, of course, was no longer on the altar before me – as it is in such blessed fashion again now – but was within me.

I had wondered if I could find you when you were not so really present as you are in the Sacrament (especially when exposed), but still you were faithful – still you are present, everywhere. And so I suppose the question arises once more as to the direction this writing should take: Should I continue to write only here before you present on the altar (up close where there is nothing between us), or take it beyond these walls?

The discovery of this way into your presence, that by recognizing what is present outside I may find what is present inside, is a marvelous revelation, I think. It is a more practical means to coming into your presence. Certainly speaking your NAME is a great gift, as is receiving and adoring your Sacrament... but this seems a way to appreciate these gifts, to find them present in my day.

And so by our senses we can indeed draw closer to you who are beyond our senses yet permeate all sense, all Creation, with your presence.

Elimination and Illumination

This naming of things, taking general account of them, serves both an eliminative and illuminative purpose. As one recognizes things – never focusing too closely on them (lest one be distracted by them) – they are in one sense eliminated, in that it becomes apparent that they themselves are not God; and also illuminated, in that by the elimination (by acknowledging what He is not) one draws closer to God, closer to the illumination found in God's presence... and then the things, too, take on a certain illumination, as reflections of the light of God shining through them.

All is of God and God is everywhere and in all things, but He Himself is none of these things. So we must discover God apart from all things (for He transcends all things), and then we will see that His light indeed shines in all things.

We may fly to the heights of the heavens or sink to the depths of the sea, but wherever we go, God is present. We cannot escape His love. Yet to discover that love, and that His love encompasses all, we must leave all of this world behind.

(It should be noted that these two actions may occur simultaneously, or either may precede or flow from the other. One may experience the illumination of things from the first, though it must always be differentiated from its source.)

Close Your Eyes

The LORD instructs me to close my eyes as I leave here, as I slowly back away from His presence on the altar, and out the door. I do not want to leave here, am inclined to stay, knowing that this is the place He is most present. But I have to go. And I seem to lose Him.

But He tells me now to close my eyes, that I might come to realize He is within me, that truly we are His tabernacles and so carry Him with us wherever we go. And there is a measure of light in my person as I do find a sense of His presence with me and begin to believe that I can bring that light outside these doors.

And so I am not so sad at leaving; I find a joy at coming to know that He is always with me. For which is greater, to be with Him, near Him on the altar, or to have Him dwelling within us, becoming one with Him?

I do not want to close my eyes, for then I will no longer see Him before me... but His grace is with me and His instruction is true, and He always has our best interest at heart. And so in being obedient to His Word I find greater blessing, something I would not have thought possible.

(But I am still here before Him as I write.)

Against the Glass

O LORD, I sit here as if with face pressed against the glass of this monstrance before me, gazing at your presence on the other side, and I wonder how I can draw closer to you and your light. How can I become one with you, dear God?

It would seem I could get no closer; it would seem I have done all I can. But I know you offer yourself even to be eaten, that you would come and dwell within man.

And so I try to remember that I have received you, indeed that I receive you each day, that you enter through the door of my mouth and find a place inside of me. If I could but remember, if I could be a member of your Body, then I would be closer to you even than when my face is pressed against the glass.

But I am so forgetful. Remind me by your breath, O LORD. Open my eyes that I may see beyond this glass into your heart.

Let my mind shine with your light and I shall not be separated from you.

Holy Spirit

I believe it is the Holy Spirit who is principally behind this third way to the presence of God, that is, through the living, illuminated senses. This is particularly true if the mind may be especially consecrated to the Holy Spirit, as I have been doing daily for some years (soul to the Father, heart to the Son... body to Mary, Our Mother).

I do find the fire of the Holy Spirit in all the light that shines around me, in all I see, in all I perceive with my senses with an illumined mind. We know that the presence of God fills the earth, that His light covers all Creation as water the sea, and this Wisdom of the LORD that infuses all seems to me the light of the Holy Spirit; I see that one can indeed consecrate one's mind to Him and so find His presence in all one perceives.

It is a most remarkable blessing and completes a kind of Trinity of paths to God, to entering His holy presence: by the NAME of the Father, by the Body and Blood of the Son, and by the Light of the Holy Spirit. And that light is reflected in a very real way in a mind on fire with the Spirit (were there not tongues of flame above the apostles' heads at Pentecost?), and by the perceptions that come therefrom. He is indeed in all things.

O LORD, let me be so surrounded by your light that I cannot escape perception of your presence in all things, that I shall fear nothing as I am enveloped by your love.

Mary

As I come to appreciate the great gift of these three ways to you, O LORD, I wonder about a fourth. Specifically, I wonder about Mary and the consecration of (especially) my body to her. Is this a fourth way to your presence?

I think of how Mary was assumed body and soul into Heaven and I wonder if the grace you give me could reach even to my flesh – could even it enter your presence? My mind may be illumined by the Spirit and so my senses serve to perceive your presence... but could the body itself be so blessed?

I think, too, of all the saints whose bodies have been found incorrupt years, even centuries, after their death. And so I wonder: could I indeed become flesh of your flesh and so find that this flesh does not rot away? This would seem to me the ultimate blessing. (Your presence would then encompass all my being.)

I cannot be so bold to ask, but if it be in your will I pray I shall accept such blessing from your hand, knowing always it is only by your grace any blessing comes to us.

Would you teach me more of this fourth way into your presence, LORD?

Bones

There is something about our bones. Even if our body, our flesh, does not last, our bones do. There is something of eternity in them.

We know from Ezekiel that even if only dry bones remain, the body can be resurrected – flesh and sinew and skin can come upon them as they draw together, and breath enter into nostrils once more... and on our feet we may stand again. There is something eternal about our bones.

Even something spiritual, I would say. Or at least it seems so to me. Ezekiel 37:5 says the Spirit comes into the bones. What exactly this means, I cannot say... But if flesh can be inviolable in Our Lady and among many saints, certainly the bones, too, remain, and could be brought to Heaven from this plane.

As I say, they last beyond the body. These white bones I feel even as I sit here and write, moving my hand and arm across the page. It is these that are at our core, that are our marrow.

O LORD, most especially I entrust my bones to your care, to your Spirit, that not one of them may be broken, that I might count them all in the Kingdom of Heaven.

Holy Thursday

O Lord, it is Holy Thursday night and I am sitting before you again. Though you are not exposed for my eyes to see, yet you are present on the altar, and I am drawn to you all the same.

It is Holy Thursday, the night your Passion begins, and I feel our salvation at hand. I could never be with you in the Garden, I could never stay awake and know what you knew this night, for the pain is beyond my understanding… and something that can be felt by no man.

Thus did your apostles fall asleep. Thus do we all sleep, O Lord. How can we stay awake in your presence: how can we know what you know?

We cannot, and you know this. And so you have mercy on our souls; and so you die for our sins.

And so, this night they come to capture you. And so, you are condemned. And on the morrow you shall be crucified. But this night you leave with us your presence on the altar. And for this, how can we thank you enough?

To the Ground

In a dream (Easter night) I seem to hear the Blessed Mother tell me that my love must reach "to the ground." I take this to mean it must become real, that it must take on flesh. It is from the ground our flesh is formed, and so even so deeply must our love go; and of course it must have the humility one finds sitting in the dust.

I sit on the ground here before our LORD on this Easter Tuesday, but I know that still I am far from the love of God, far from being flesh of the flesh of Christ and of Our Lady. It is reported that this month's message from Medjugorje tells us how far we are from the love of God, and how far we must come… and the words ring true in my soul.

To the ground. O LORD, when will your love become so real in my life? For even on Easter Monday, temptations are upon me, and I am yet so lazy and weak.

How shall this flesh be as your own – how shall I enter your presence?

Sometimes it seems it cannot be done, but I must have faith and learn to sacrifice for your sake. (Help me, dearest LORD.)

Time Stands Still

O LORD, here before your presence time stands still and we step into eternal life. There is no movement, there is no sound, and no time passes. A thousand years, a single day, what difference does it make? An hour or a minute, it doesn't matter, for we are in your presence, and all is but one moment. The moment is all we have, for in the moment you dwell, and you are Life itself.

How literally we sense the stillness of time in your presence: sometimes it seems as if we have been with you an hour when only a few minutes have passed; other times it seems only minutes when hours have gone by... Does this not show us that time does not matter with you?

But how shall we come to dwell in eternity with you, O LORD? When will it be we never leave your presence? Truly your presence is with us at all times (or no time would exist), but how shall we come to be with you, to remember your presence with us?

O let time stand still in our hearts!

Flesh of Christ

The crucifix above the altar is so real. The corpus is larger than life and His flesh indeed seems so tangible. The wounds on His body are evident – the lacerations, the blood upon hands and feet and side, the darkened knees... Truly it seems I could reach out and touch Him, and hold Him in my arms.

Just so real should our own flesh be, so reflective of our Lord. In our own hands let us carry His wounds and walk always in His stead. As real as the Bread beneath the crucifix should be our lives in Christ.

We consume His Body and Blood, do we not? We partake every day of this Food. Let it be who we become; let us be flesh of His flesh and bone of His bone. So wed should we be to Him that we are truly one.

O Lord, let your blood pour upon me from this Tree; let me embrace your tortured flesh. Your suffering let us carry about in our own bodies, and so become one with you.

This wood is the path to the flesh of Christ, to living as His disciples.

Priests

There are few people in the chapel, but two of them today are priests – a special blessing.

Jesus, how blessed are the souls who stand in your place at the altar and serve to bring your presence to us. Where would we be without them? We would be without you and your real presence.

On the night you were betrayed you took bread and wine in your sacred hands and lifted them up to the Father, and they became your Body and Blood. As at the Father's Word the universe was made, so at your Word you remain with us in this Sacrament. And it is your priests who speak your words today, who consecrate the bread and wine as you have commanded.

And so you never leave. In this very real way indeed you remain. Certainly your Spirit is upon us and inspires all who call on your Name in truth... but your flesh and blood we cannot bring to this earth, however inspired our words might be – only your priests can do this.

And so, how blessed we are to have them in our midst this day.

The Annunciation

O Jesus, your Mother spoke with the Angel, communicated with him eye to eye, heart to heart... In her the divine and the human meet and are made one, by your grace, O Lord. At the end of their encounter she is no longer afraid but in complete union with the will of the Father, and in His presence she is at home.

O how your light illumines her mind! How you open her eyes to see God, to know God... to bear you within her womb. Why should it be remarkable that the one who bears God to the world should communicate with angels? Yet its marvel stirs my soul to tears.

O Mother, pray for us this day and every day that we shall be so open to the will of the LORD that we will hear His Word and be able to look His messenger in the eye... that His light will fill our minds also. Pray we shall follow in your way and so find union with the LORD as you have done.

Even unto death I give my life to you, O LORD, through the Blessed Mother. I pray my sacrifice will be acceptable to you and union with you I too will discover, by your grace and mercy.

Speak, LORD, your servant is listening.

Lead me in your way.

My Heart Beating

I look upon the flowers before the altar and the brick of the back wall, the flickering candles and the glint of light off the golden monstrance... but I find you most, Lord, in my heart beating – here is your presence clearest to me. And through my heart beating I find you also in the flowers and the brick and the flickering light; if you are in me, I can see you in all things. If you are not in me, how can I see you anywhere? For then I am blind.

But as it is my heart is beating and I can sense you present there within, my soul graced by your love, graced by your Sacrament, graced by your will to share with me your presence everywhere. And so I cannot escape you. And so I am surrounded, encompassed by your light.

And in this I can but rejoice. And the closer you come, the more joyful I am... though the joy is not without fear, or without pain. For the closer you come, the more wonderful is your presence – and how much can my poor human soul bear of your immeasurable love?

But I beg you never to leave, never to cease drawing closer to my heart, that it shall someday beat with your love alone, in the presence of the Father.

(O Mother Mary, pray for us.)

Never Leave

As I hear the door close (lightly) behind a soul leaving the chapel, I wonder why any of us would go outside this house, outside this refuge where Jesus is so present. Why should we ever leave?

And yet I know that I too will return to the noise outside these doors, where music blares from passing cars and engines run nonstop. I will soon be there.

But again I must ask the LORD that somehow I never leave, that here I shall stay, remembering Him always, even to my bones – that my heart shall never stop beating with His own.

Soon the time will come, and soon I will be distracted (it seems now the noise has even entered inside these walls, as some electronic device speaks up); it is inevitable, I'm afraid. Maybe someday I shall remain here in His presence all the day, even on this soiled earth… but now I know that soon I shall go forth into the world.

Let me not be afraid, O LORD. Let me not doubt that with me you can remain, even in the midst of the noise. O please let it be that I shall never leave!

It can be so. It is so. If only we could see. If only we could breathe as one with Him who rises far above our reality.

What Is Not Present

O LORD, what is not present to you? Evil. Evil alone is not in your midst, for how can that which is against you be a part of you? Evil by definition is that which is separated from you (a deformation of your goodness) and has no place in your Kingdom.

And so, let us turn from every evil, and toward every good thing – let us turn always toward your light, toward the light of the Spirit shining in our minds by the grace that comes to us only through you and your love. Let this light be our guide.

And then, indeed, all things will be blessed by you; all things will be present to you and with you, for all things will be illumined by your Spirit, O holy God. (Then, indeed, we shall never leave your presence.)

Evil, we should say, is not present at all, is not real at all – it is only of chaos and darkness, which are empty and fated for destruction when the glance of the LORD strikes them. They cannot stand. They will not last for they cannot remain in the light of the LORD. They soon will be no more.

(Let all evil pass from you, my son.)

Reconciler of Opposites

Only God could take the most disparate of things and bring them into harmonious union; only He could make one what seem most opposed. For what are more opposed than the infinite God and finite man; what could be further apart? Yet in Christ the two meet and kiss, for He is truly divine and truly human.

And if the divine and human can be thus reconciled, what is there beyond the LORD's power to unite? Thus, in Him falls all division between Jew and Gentile, between warring parties of any kind, for in Him there is but peace, and that peace is eternal.

And so the false dichotomies of this world fade away, have all their vanity exposed in this true light; and so all the self-serving differences man concocts between himself and his neighbor indeed fall by the wayside, and return to dust.

And so, that which seems most impossible – that we poor humans could enter the presence of God and become one with Him who made us and redeems us from our sin – now becomes quite real before our eyes, now walks among us and beats in our hearts. Let us praise the living God!

SILENCE

YHWH, how pregnant your Silence is with the Truth – we hear all things in your silent presence. Here there are no distractions; indeed, these fall silent before you. As there was silence in Heaven for half an hour at the opening of the seventh seal, so all the universe falls silent before you and Truth is known: it is then it is spoken most clearly.

And you call us to silence now, to silence our machines and our feet, our hearts and our lungs… To breathe as one with you who are eternal, we must silence all that is of this world. There is no other way to your Kingdom, to your Truth.

How blessed is this Silence, LORD, which we too infrequently hear, for which we rarely listen. Change our hearts and our minds that being in your presence will be our greatest wish, our most sincere desire. Then we shall not fail to come to you.

Speak your Silence clearly to us, that we might not mistake your presence or wander aimlessly from your love.

SILENCE – listen to the LORD.

Remind Me

Remind me of your presence within me, LORD. As I kneel here before you in the Sacrament, remind me that I have partaken of this same Sacrament and that you are therefore within me now. Bring to my mind the blessing this is, how really you make yourself one with me. For I have eaten your Body and drunk your Blood, and so indeed I have life in me.

So many there are who do not know this power; so many are so apart from you. And even if they love your Word and praise you as God, still, without your Body and Blood they do not have you so present within. And should I forget that I receive you each day?

Truly we can be vain, empty of your presence, even if we eat and drink of you every day. How terrible to receive you in vain! And so, how I must beg you indeed to remind me of the gift I have, remind me of your presence within, that I shall remember always I am part of your Body on this earth.

Let your power be known through me as you bless me with remembrance of your gifts and graces. Let them ever grow and become a holy sacrifice unto your NAME.

Light to My Mind

O LORD, how you bring light to my mind! Even if I am tired and weak, when I come close to you here, you awaken my mind and enliven my soul. And how overwhelming your light can become! It leaves me in a kind of dizziness at your awesome presence.

O the Light! When we open our eyes wide and begin to see, to realize that your light is shining before us at all times – indeed, how our mind can be overwhelmed! How can we bear such glory; how can we remain in your light?

Even when my eyes are closed, your light overwhelms me, for even then I can look up to you and see your glory shining. Help me, O LORD, to bear this blessing by your grace and never waste the blessing, never turn from your light.

O how I forget you, LORD! O how blind my eyes can be most of the time! Help me to come into your presence and there remain with you.

Surround me with your light and let me not escape its glory... Somehow make it my constant companion, that I might always remember you.

In Heaven

Are we not in Heaven as Jesus comes to us and makes His home in us when we receive Him present in the Blessed Sacrament? Does He not here in our heart prepare a room for us in His Father's House? Are we not His temple?

Do we not overhear His conversation with His Mother and see the angels standing round praising the LORD our God? Do we not join in their chorus?

He comes to us. He makes His home in us. We eat His Body and drink His Blood and so are made one with Him who is Heaven itself; and so it is in Heaven, with Heaven, we dwell when we receive Him worthily in Holy Communion. And then our hearts are not troubled. And then we are at peace. For then we are in His presence.

And is this room, this chapel, not like the room He prepares for us within our hearts? Is He not here in this place, present to us on the altar, making Himself known to every open eye and heart? This is His temple, too. And through this temple He calls us to become His temple.

When you receive the Lord, realize what it is you do. Do not partake of His Body and Blood without discerning His presence. And know that hereby you come to Heaven. Realize how greatly you are blessed.

Heart Aflame

O Lord, let my heart be aflame with your blood, with your love, and not cold and hard as it has become. Let my soul be on fire to proclaim your praise.

O Lord, let your flame rise up in my heart, in my soul, in my mind, that I might be alive in your love and become one with you. O leave me not empty and alone!

How your heart burns with love for us; how willing you are to lay down your life – how you bleed for us, dear Lord. And we, what do we do for you? We, in turn, readily shun your Cross.

O Lord, let me embrace your Cross and then indeed my heart will burn with your love; then indeed I will be aflame in your presence forevermore. Take me from my selfishness to dwell with you.

All your saints have their hearts afire in your glory, dear God. All your angels are like ministering flames of your love. Let us join with them even here on earth that our place in Heaven will be assured. Set our hearts on fire with your Spirit, Lord.

Words

O LORD, sometimes it seems all I have is words, just words, and I wonder why I continue to speak, why I continue to write – should I not rather fall silent? My prayer is that somehow you are in these words giving them light, and that somehow they shall have some good purpose. But sometimes it seems all I have is words.

So many words. And what good are they if spoken in vain? How can they bring us into your presence? (And all that matters is that we come into your presence.) On the page they are indeed dead; O let them not be dead in my heart!

On I go. Should I stop, O LORD? Should I put my pen aside? Who will read these words and what purpose have they? But still I find your hand upon me and see your light shining about me... and so, on I go.

Guide me, please, I beg, O LORD. Always guide my words – every thought, every breath, every word I write (or speak).

Let there be some good in these words… or else, indeed, lead me to put down my pen.

YHWH

It always comes back to your NAME, O LORD, to your Silence, to your Presence… There is nothing else, nothing else that is real; nothing matters apart from you.

And I remember how I can always and everywhere come into your presence by speaking your NAME: "YHWH." When I do, my mind is immediately filled with light and I am alive, and I am with you. This is all that matters – and how close you are!

But how easily and often I forget. And so, how desperately and eternally I need to remember. For in this alone is grace – we must *be* in your presence.

O let your Silence fall upon me and nurture me, dear God. Let it fill me completely with remembrance of you. If I were filled with your light from head to toe and fingertips to fingertips, nothing else would I need in this world… for I would already be present in the next.

Let me stop speaking now. Let your Silence fill my soul. Let me be in your presence, LORD, now and forevermore. (O let me remember your NAME!)

2

LOVE
THY
ENEMY

(On the Passion of Christ and Its Place in the World)

The silent NAME of the LORD (YHWH) is remembered best by Christ on the Cross – here the NAME is spoken perfectly. And so if we wish to enter the presence of the LORD, to remember His NAME always, as we say we do, then we must of necessity embrace the Cross. And we embrace the Cross in the most substantial manner when we love our enemies.

Our enemies may be any number of things: people who persecute us, situations that try us, a world which opposes us at every turn and would draw us into its grasp... In all things we are called to love, and called especially by Christ in His ultimate teaching to love those who most challenge us. This is His way: to come to the Father we must be like the Father who shines His light on the evil and the good. And it is in shining light on the evil we are pierced as Jesus and come most directly to the Father.

How Jesus' silence on the Cross should speak to us!

God Is Love

If God is love then what can He do but love; and if we are of God what should *we* do but love? Our lives should be entirely of charity, with no room for anything but love. If there is anger or impatience in us, if we look upon others with judgment in our hearts, how are we reflective of God, how are we Christian? No, God is love and anything that is not of love is not of God.

Thus we are called to love even our enemies, because we can be of nothing but love, nothing but God. There must be no evil in us at all, and so we cannot meet evil with evil and say we are disciples of Christ. Jesus does not do this and He insists His disciples be like Him (or they are not His disciples).

Do we want to find God? Do we want to be followers of the Lord Jesus? If we realize what a blessing it is to become like God, then we will not find it difficult or rebel against the call to love our enemies – we will embrace it with the greatest joy.

God is love. This is all we need to know. God is love and is only of love. And we must be as He is or we fall short of His call and the great grace He would pour upon our souls.

Generosity

The Psalms tell us the just man is generous and lends; he is never lacking in goods to share with others and gives them freely. The Lord tells us that from the store of the heart the mouth speaks and that we cannot give what we do not have: a good tree bears good fruit and a rotten one bad fruit. This is clear logic.

And God is the most generous of all – He is the source of all generosity for He owns the world and all it holds and shares it with whomever He will. And so, what is the just man but an image of God, reflecting His generosity. But he could not be so generous unless blessed first by the LORD; and he could not be so generous (or blessed) if his heart was not so willing to share.

His heart is open, and so the LORD places in it good things, that he might share them with all. He indeed is the image of God, His child, His heir, both of the love only He holds and the goods of this world.

Blessed are the merciful for they shall obtain mercy. How can one find mercy if his heart is closed? And so, let us be of the mercy of God.

We Only Lend

We can only lend, for we do not own anything, not even our lives. Nothing is ours to give, for all belongs to God.

But He places in our hands our lives and all the things He shares with us that we might show ourselves as openhanded as He and prove worthy of His love, of His greatest blessing: eternal life. This above all is not our own; it is a gift from our Creator.

And from our Redeemer. For we had lost even what we thought we had, what had been ours for a time... and so were left with nothing. So lost were we, we had nothing even to lend another – we were indeed empty and vain.

Now that we are redeemed, grace works within us again and so we participate in the generosity of our LORD, in the exchange of goods, spiritual goods. But still, we only lend what is His alone.

And so all things let us lay at His feet, all our works and all our prayers and even our very lives, and allow His mercy to work in us for the good of everyone.

Mercy

What is God to us but mercy? For far, far above us He dwells, and His ways are beyond our understanding; yet He reaches down to us and touches us, and draws us unto Himself. This is pure mercy for our souls.

We cannot begin to look upon the LORD, to know of His presence, without first knowing of His mercy, without first experiencing the grace that flows from Him; for it is so, that He loved us first, that while we were still sinners He sent His Son among us to turn our hearts to Him. Without this grace, without the outpouring of His merciful heart, we would be forever lost in darkness.

The world is in darkness; we are blind and without hope. But He who is light comes to us and opens our eyes to His presence, to His glory... and we become filled with light. If we do not recognize the darkness of the world in which we live, we shall never come to His light, for we will have no need of His mercy, and so will never know Him.

O LORD, let your mercy make our hearts beat with your love that we might praise you in all things.

In Praise

In praise we know Him for in praise we know ourselves and our place before Him Who made us, Who deserves our praise. And so, fulfilling this innate call of our souls to offer Him praise, we become who we are, children of God, and so come to know the Father.

And so, let us praise the LORD our God with all our being, with all our heart, mind, soul, and strength; then fully will we know Him; then fully will we find our place before Him and look upon Him with love, the same love He has for us, for His children.

How grateful we should be to be alive, to have come into the light of His day. How grateful we should be for the mercy of the One Who made us, Who from nothing caused us to be. And so, let us be; let us be the children we were made to be and give thanks and praise, due honor to our God.

Jesus praised the Father even from the Cross. He was obedient to Him in love even unto death, never failing of the praise we should all have for all things in our lives; for all is in the Father's hands and He takes care of all. Even from the Cross let us praise the LORD and we will be joined to Jesus and so to the Father.

The Darkest Hour

In your darkest hour do not fail to praise the LORD and He will not fail to pour the light of His presence upon your soul. And so you will be set free from your darkest hour.

There is no darkness in Him at all – all is light in His holy presence. And to that presence He cannot but draw you if you but praise and glorify His NAME, if you but follow His command of love. Do not let the darkness overcome you. Hold on to His light.

Even if you can barely pry open your mouth, even if it seems you have nothing to say… speak His NAME, praise His glory, and He will do the rest. Trust in Him. It will not fail you.

All is founded on our trust in the LORD, on our faith. And all is possible to those who believe. O LORD, we believe; help our unbelief! Fill our eyes and our minds with your holy light that shines so brightly this day before your altar as we bask in the presence of your Sacrament. Teach us to love as you love. Teach us always to love.

Our Greatest Enemy

Our greatest enemy is death, and yet it serves as the great equalizer of all men, and in Christ brings great peace.

There is nothing man fears more than his own mortality and its inevitability. There is nothing man in all his technological prowess can do to prevent what comes to all of us… and how this harrows the soul without faith!

Death will be the last enemy placed beneath the feet of Jesus in His eternal rule. Until that time it shall remain as a curse, and blessing, from the LORD.

Every enemy we must love, and so most certainly we must love our greatest enemy; and in the love of our greatest enemy we find the greatest blessing, the greatest love and life without end. And so, how much we need to turn this curse to a blessing for our souls!

It is not an easy enemy to overcome by love, and many paths we may walk mistakenly on this journey. For death itself is indeed a curse, and so suicide is no solution. We must embrace only life, for only life is in the LORD. But in the LORD even this curse becomes a blessing, as united with Christ we conquer the world and escape its hold. Once our fear of death is overcome by the grace of God, there is nothing left to fear – only love remains.

Tears of Humility

How can we even raise our eyes to you, O LORD? Should we not remain always on our knees with our heads to the ground? How can we presume to judge our neighbor, arrogating to ourselves your domain? O give us tears of humility to serve as balm for our souls – let our hearts be torn in two before you.

It is only by your grace we raise our heads at all, only by your favor that we can praise you. But do we turn to you for such favor, or do we prefer to take pride in what is our own? How foolish we can be, LORD, how blind, how deaf... What can save us but your intercession, your reaching down to touch our hearts?

David was graced with tears and cleansed thereby of his sins... Every repentant soul you would save. O let us not fail of repentance for our sin; let us never find no need of repentance! For then we would be condemned, as indeed we are as we dally in our sin.

Turn the piercing fire upon your own soul, my brother. Fail not to accept chastisement. How can you begin to love your enemy if you see not the sin within yourself?

The Encroaching Darkness

There is a darkness falling upon the earth. It is deep and abiding. There is no escaping its reach except by the way of Christ, except by His Cross and our embracing it thoroughly. Only if we die in Him will we be saved.

This encroaching darkness is terrible, a horror to behold. And it is reflective of the sin within us all. In a word, it is evil. The devil has his grip upon this world and he shall not release it easily. We must repent entirely of the hold he has upon us.

And we cannot pretend there is no darkness in us; then we would be liars (as John has made clear) and our salvation would be far away. No, we must rend our hearts, fall to our knees, and beg the LORD as the worst of sinners we are (all of us), and then His mercy may overshadow the darkness – then His light will come.

But let us be sincere or the encroaching darkness will consume our souls and we shall die in our pride, and not with Christ.

O LORD, let my blood be poured forth only for your sake and for the salvation of souls, even the darkest among us.

The Increasing Light

Even as the darkness encroaches, the light increases; and this light comes through the darkness, through the darkest deed done by man, through our crucified Lord.

O how the light pours forth from the Cross! O how the grace of God comes from His wounds! And how great that light is, that light that not only cannot be conquered by darkness but turns darkness to light. That light will be all that is on the last day.

And until that day it shall ever increase, despite the darkness and destroying the darkness. It shines from the Cross of Christ and shall continue so till the end of time through all those who follow in His steps.

O how the LORD blesses us! For we indeed carry His light forth. We indeed conquer the darkness of this earth, of this world lost in sin and disobedience to the will of God. And we shall never be conquered, for we indeed are with the Christ and share in the glory of His sacrifice. Alleluia!

Let Me Dwell in Your Wounds

Let me dwell in your wounds, O Lord, and there take my refuge, for in them is sweetness, despite the suffering wrought by the world.

Sometimes the world weighs upon us; sometimes we are blessed to suffer with Christ because of our faithfulness to His Word, to His command to love. But the pain that comes is tenderly assuaged by the wounds of our God and our dwelling there with Him. O how sweet it is!

Here indeed we find a home, a place where the Father's arms embrace us and comfort us as no mother can. Here there is peace, peace that passes understanding as it passes beyond any suffering. For, indeed, in this place we are home.

His wounds bleed so tenderly, with the deepest love and sympathy for any pain we might feel, and indeed transform our suffering into an abiding joy in the presence of the LORD. Do not be afraid to enter there, for then you will be carried far from here, though very much here you remain.

Let me dwell in your wounds, O Lord, and so find the peace of Heaven when suffering is upon me. (And let me not fail to suffer with you.)

Your Blood Be upon These Pages

Cover me with your blood, O LORD; your Spirit be in these words. Your blood be upon these pages or they will be worth nothing.

If we are to love our enemy, then we must love our most troublesome foe: ourselves. For who stands more in the way of our coming to the LORD and His light than we ourselves, and so who needs more the mercy of Christ?

We must take the blood of Christ upon our souls, recognizing clearly our role in His death, if we are to find His blood upon us for good, if we are to discover the salvation it has wrought. There is no other way to Heaven.

If we forget His blood, if we do not ascribe to ourselves our outstanding guilt... of what good is anything we do – what purpose would there be to anything I write?

His blood must course through our veins if the Spirit is to speak through us. The blood and the Spirit must both testify or our words are but a clanging gong.

O let my heart not be empty of your sacrifice, for only in love do we find our call and come to your Paradise.

Unbounded Joy

There is unbounded joy in your presence, O LORD, and we come to this joy when we conquer the world, as your Son has done through the grace of the Cross. And then there is only praise of your NAME.

When the world has no hold over us, when all fear has fled our hearts and only love remains, when we realize that love cannot be conquered by anything the devil throws our way – then what is left but to praise the LORD with an unending joy. The chains of the devil broken, we sing the praise of God.

And this freedom comes when we love our enemy, when we love all and everything – when we recognize that all is in the hand of God and He always watches over, then nothing stands in the way of love and joy. We can turn the other cheek, we can go the extra mile... we can take any temptation that comes our way and turn it back upon Satan with a smile.

Alleluia, praise the LORD! For He is mighty and has done great things. And the greatest of these is our salvation in the blood of His only Son, by our sharing in that blood. What can we do but rejoice?

The Visitation

Across the hills her feet fly to the side of her sister; there she opens the curtains of time, letting the light of the LORD shine upon the face of Elizabeth. And Elizabeth awakens as the child in her womb stirs for the first time, leaping in joy at Mary's voice, at the very presence of God. And in the Spirit they praise YHWH.

Does the LORD not love His enemy (Rm.5:8-10)? Does He not come to us in our desperation, in the darkness of this forsaken world, and seek to save our souls? Though it brings Him straight to the Cross, He does not hesitate to enter our midst and subject Himself to our sin.

How sweet is His coming! How blessed is she who carries Him to us without a care for herself. She is like Him. Her heart is poured out for the sake of others even as her Son. And O how we must be the same!

He has come freely among us and taken the Cross upon Himself, and we must freely join Him, following in the wake of our Mother.

The Face of Esau

In the face of Esau, Jacob saw his brother, he saw the LORD, he saw the angel he had wrestled with the night before... he saw his enemy and he saw himself, and all his fear departed.

If we have eyes illumined by God, then we will see Him present in all things, and especially in the face of our brother; the face of YHWH will be unmistakable, even if our brother is our enemy, even if he seeks to take our life. For the light of the LORD illumines even this face – it illumines even our own.

Jacob looked in the mirror and saw his enemy was himself, and that God was present to illumine him, to banish all darkness from his heart. And so he saw God in the face of Esau. And how it astounded him!

Throughout the night he had wrestled with the LORD, with His angel... and with his brother and himself. He showed the strength of God, for God's strength was upon him, blessing him in his struggle. And when morning came he was given a new name. He would be Jacob no more, no longer set on supplanting his brother – he would be Israel, he in whom all nations find their blessing.

There Is Nowhere God Is Not

It is impossible for God not to be, for He is Being itself – He is the great I AM. And so, anywhere you are, God is there. Of this you should be assured and you will be greatly blessed.

And with this assurance in your soul, you will know you have nothing to fear... for you are never apart from God. Unless of course you do not wish to be with God, then there is much to fear – indeed, hell itself. For you shall not escape Him.

Certainly there should be a holy fear, a holy reverence for the greatness of the LORD and our own smallness before Him – and this blessed fear should never leave us. But this fear leads only to

His love wrapping us in its light and peace. And what fear can there be in that?

There is nowhere God is not. What a blessed thought, what a blessed realization of the presence of God and of His encompassing love, a love that destroys by its grace all fear of any enemy and replaces it with joy.

You are of God, my brother, whoever you are.

He Is Nowhere More Than Here

Jesus is with us on this earth, this soiled earth, and He is nowhere more present on this earth than in the Blessed Sacrament now before me on the altar. And so I am in the place He most is. What a blessing is upon me! And upon all who adore Him here.

And what of those who receive Him, even every day? How could they be more blessed than this? On this earth it is not possible to imagine a greater blessing than is ours each day.

For, indeed, He is nowhere more than here. Though God is everywhere and in everything, especially since the Incarnation of the Son, that Incarnation is known to us in no greater way than by the grace of the Sacrament He left with us on the night He was betrayed. How real is His presence here!

When we reach Heaven where God is all that Is, His presence here will be exceeded by His encompassing presence there... but while we are on this soiled earth, how blessed we are to be in this place that has no compare. O Jesus, in your presence let us be forever!

Joseph Weeps

Like the heavy rain that beats down on the roof of this Florida chapel, so Joseph wept in the presence of his brothers (who had sold him into slavery), loud enough for all Egypt to hear. And as the silence that comes when the rain suddenly stops, so is the peace that possesses him as he throws his arms around them. He is home.

As great as is the blessing the LORD provides in making him ruler over all of Egypt, as much honor and power as he enjoyed (and as much good as he was able to do), still he was a Hebrew in a foreign land… and it all meant nothing till his brothers returned.

And he suffers all for the sake of his kin, accepts his being sold into slavery and living in exile as the will of God, seeing only the good that comes of it now that he can provide for his family.

And so his family shall prosper. And so the Israelites will become numerous in the land and spread across the face of the earth, a blessing to all nations. And so Joseph fulfills his call by the grace of the LORD. And so he is welcomed home.

Forgiveness

How blessed is forgiveness! The Lord has told us it is our means to salvation, and truly it is, for it brings the release of all bitterness from our hearts. And it allows us to see how all things are indeed in the hand of God and nothing happens without His approval, or without bringing blessing. So even the most terrible trials we suffer (perhaps these more than anything else) are means to glory.

How blessed we are when indeed we begin to see the hand of the LORD at work in our enemies! And how blessed we shall thus be in Heaven. O when our hearts bleed for those who harm us, when we weep upon their shoulders as upon the shoulder of a brother... then we have the heart of Jesus; then we enter the realm of Heaven.

Here is truly our salvation: unless you forgive, you will not be forgiven; but he who forgives his brother from his heart, all goodness is his in the arms of the LORD. Then he becomes a child of God.

We must reflect the glory of our Father; we must be as He is. His love knows no bounds and neither should our own. All must be as our brother.

Jesus Weeps

Jesus weeps. What can He do but weep? When He looks upon Jerusalem in her sin, when He looks upon each of us whom He would save, what can He do but mourn our spurning of His love? And so, Jesus weeps.

For, indeed, He loves us. He loves us as His children; He loves us as He loves Himself, and there is nothing He would not give to see us turn to Him and receive His love and live as His children. But what do we do but turn away? And so, what can He do but weep over us?

His heart bleeds for us, His will is to redeem us... but He cannot force Himself upon us, He cannot make us love Him (for we are free to choose as we please). And so, all He can do He does: He stretches His arms out on the Cross to receive all our hatred and pain – all our sin.

But will this satisfy us? Will this cause us to seek to wipe His tears? Or will His weeping be ignored?

Our souls need His tears. His tears wash clean all who come to them, all who taste their salt. Let His blood pour upon you, my brother, that into His arms you may come.

"They Know Not What They Do"

Jesus not only forgives us, He advocates on our behalf, even as He bleeds and dies on the Cross from wounds inflicted by our sins. He makes excuse for us that we might be saved from actions that merit death.

When we love our enemies, whom do we love but ourselves, for who among us is not a sinner deserving condemnation? Indeed, we are all sinners, none able to judge another but all called to forgive one another if we hope to be forgiven. This is indeed a requisite of our salvation: that we forgive others. Else we shall not be forgiven.

And so we must love all, we must forgive all, whether it be terrorists planting bombs to destroy us, those engaging in grave sexual sin, or souls who stand in judgment of every wrong. We are called to love them all, for there is nothing else we can do. For to condemn anyone would be to condemn ourselves.

We must indeed presume they know not what they do. As grave as their (or our) sin may be, we cannot know if they act with full knowledge and clear consent of the will. Indeed, many claim to be doing the right thing: they say they love, they believe they are doing God's will... they think they are justified. They know not what they do.

This is our prayer for them, as for ourselves: *they know not what they do.* May all be saved. (This is God's will.)

God's Will

It is indeed God's will that all men be saved, and it is God's will Jesus accomplishes on the Cross: here is our salvation wrought, here in His blood, in His blessed sacrifice for our sakes.

How could the Father will such a thing for His Son, that He should be crucified like a criminal though innocent of any wrong? He does so for you who ask this question – His heart bleeds for you, and no sacrifice is too great for His children.

And Jesus is a willing participant; He knows what blessing will come by the laying down of His life – it is indeed for our sakes He dies, for He loves us like the Father. (Should He possess less love? Should He not care as He does?)

And what of us who call ourselves Christians, who seek to walk in Jesus' path? Should we have less love than the One we worship, than the One to whom we give our lives? Can we fall short of His sacrifice and call ourselves children of God?

God's will is for us as well: the same love He would have us know. And so He calls us to lay down our lives as the Lamb has done.

The Lamb

How gentle is the Lamb, how meek and how humble. Such is Jesus, such is our God… and such should we be, this day and always.

It is hard. It is hard to follow in the footsteps of Christ, to walk the path He has trod so perfectly in making Himself a sacrifice for our sins; for how inclined we are to defend ourselves from attacks – how difficult to turn the other cheek and remain humble before those who persecute us.

But this is what we must do. Even as the dark clouds approach on the horizon, we must remain faithful to the Lamb and His blood: we must walk His way of the Cross.

And in this we will find our salvation. The LORD will strengthen us with His peace, with His presence, and into His presence we shall come. And, please God, others shall be guided there by our example, by the grace we share with them through the power of God.

Jesus is the Lamb of God who takes away the sins of the world; if He were not gentle and humble, if He did not freely give His life, there would be no hope for any soul to overcome the darkness of this world. But as it is the Lamb is amongst us. Let His blood beat in our hearts.

Bathed in His Blood

"Washed and saved!" the ancients cried when they saw their martyrs drenched in blood by the teeth of the lions. How blessed was this bath of blood, for by such witness to the Lord indeed they were cleansed from all sin – nothing of themselves remained. They were bathed in Christ's blood and knew its grace to their bones.

O let us give all we are over to our LORD and God! Let us fully embrace the Cross even if it means shedding our own blood. There can be no greater blessing than to die with Jesus, for then we shall also live with Him, and bring others to His altar.

Here is the holiest sacrifice we can make upon this earth – the offering of our very lives for the sake of God and others. Engaged in this sacrifice, our blood mingles with Jesus' own.

O let us be bathed in His blood that we might be washed and saved and come readily into His Kingdom. Let His blood pour upon us each and every day that in His presence we shall remain and be filled with every grace and blessing. Wash us in your Blood, O Lord!

Pierce My Eyes

Pierce my eyes with your light, O LORD, and let my mind be filled with your wisdom; with your patience may I draw near to you, even on this day. O let me find the narrow gate that leads to you, and enter there by your grace.

Can we be filled with encompassing light, with a light that would blind our eyes if they were not blessed by God? Are we ready to stand in His presence; such awesome wonder can we approach in innocence, and so not be consumed? The way indeed is narrow that leads to the LORD.

And the narrow way is known best in Jesus' most challenging commandment: to love our enemies. There is nothing more difficult than this, nothing more painful, more piercing... and nothing more blessed. There is no greater love to which we may come as we tread this barren earth – it is of the love of God.

And so it brings us to God, to the LORD of all who lives in eternal glory far from our own poor dwelling place. But to Him do we come this way.

Let our eyes be pierced with His light, pierced with His tears that cleanse our eyes and prepare them for such vision... Let our tears pour forth for our enemies.

Closer to Our Lady

Closer to Our Lady I draw this day; under her mantle I come and take rest in its shade. She is our secure protection, the greatest of mothers.

And how close she has drawn to our Savior! How one with Him she has become. Flesh of her flesh He becomes, and so makes her His own. He is her beloved Son.

How close to Our Lady we should indeed draw, becoming like her who is so much like Him. She who was called from all eternity, preserved from the stain of sin, and reflective of the Lord's own humility – she should be our Model in the Faith.

The Faith finds fulfillment in this poor virgin from Palestine; the Faith of Abraham, the Faith of all ages, is present with her, and the source of that Faith is borne in her womb. No closer to Him could any of us come.

Take refuge in Mary, my brother, my sister. In her arms make your home. Then you will be joined to Jesus and become as the Father's own. Closer to her let us draw each day. There is simply no greater love.

And to Her Love

As we draw closer to Our Lady, we draw closer to her love, a love like that of God. Her love beats in a pure heart with no room for anything but love. Like the LORD – who is love and whose light shines on the evil and the good, who can do nothing but love – so is she who is joined to Him. She is one with Jesus on the Cross and can only offer love even to those who crucify her Son.

This is the love to which we are all called, the love she holds so perfectly in her soul. If we are to be sons and daughters of God, there is nothing we can do but embrace this love. (Is there anything better for which to strive?)

And she will bring us to the place where her Son dwells in perfect love, in perfect light. Even on this soiled earth we can approach such love by the grace that flows through her from the Holy Spirit. That same grace may flow through us if we open ourselves completely to God's love.

And so, let us beseech her intercession for our sakes; let us consecrate ourselves to her beloved Son by the Mother through whom He has come, and He will make His home in us as well – we will be like her, His Temple.

His Temple

His Temple is pure, it is holy; it admits of no sin, no hatred of any kind... It holds but love. And so those not of love cannot enter there.

We must be His temples, temples of the Holy Spirit, temples of His love and truth; we must keep His presence within us and allow His love to work through us.

If we receive Him every day, indeed every day do we become His tabernacles, His temples. We must not be blind to this fact or ignore the grace given us by the Lord. And so, we must be like Him. If He is with us, we cannot but be like Him, or we receive Him in vain.

O Lord, let my life not be in vain; let me not be with you and apart from you. Let me not come to your temple each day to pray and leave without your grace at work in my soul, at work in my life. Let me not receive you in vain.

Let me truly be as your Temple, carrying you wherever I go, sharing your love with all the world. Of what worth is my life if this is not so? You are my all, O Lord; let my love be true.

3

PROPHECY

The LORD speaks through His prophets
with the same Breath that moved upon the waters
before He spoke and brought Creation to Light.

To Moses He spoke face to face.
And would we doubt the Word of God?

The mouth of the prophet
opens unto eternity;
his eyes see beyond the clouds,
beyond the sky.

God is not limited by space and time
but is the Maker of space and time –
this is something we cannot see,
something we cannot believe,
and so, something we do not understand.

And so with our limited minds
we attempt to explain,
and explain away,
the Word of God,
making it conform to our limited vision.

We are thus *blind* to prophecy,
as we are blind to God.

Called into the Cloud

Like Moses we are called into the cloud on the LORD's holy mountain, where His light shines, where His glory is known. There in the cloud the LORD composed His commandments on the tablets of stone with His own finger, for there in the cloud the LORD's Word is spoken most clearly to the ears and hearts of men. It is in this cloud we must make our home, in the presence of the LORD.

When this cloud filled the tent in the desert, Moses spoke to the LORD face to face – no closer could anyone come to His presence (except by encountering Christ). And when Moses came from the sacred presence of the LORD, his face shone with glorious light, so awesome that the Israelites could not bear to look upon him. For indeed he emanated the glory of God, and how can we sinful men look upon this?

But more than look upon it we must: we must live in the overwhelming presence of the LORD – it is there we must remain. And so, how pure we must be.

We are indeed called into the cloud, into the glory of God. Will we heed His voice?

The Word of God

How many times does the Bible say, "Thus says the LORD," when a prophet is about to speak? Does this not make clear that we should receive the Word of God, "not as the word of men, but as it truly is, the Word of God" (1Thes.2:13)? Yet how little faith do even many Bible scholars put in the Word of the LORD.

All of the Bible is one Word; it is all of the Breath of God, emanating from His Mind and proclaiming one thing – that the LORD is God and that this is His NAME: YHWH. From this Silence, from this place of light, all Scripture speaks, with the mouth of a loving God.

Here we have not a work of the imagination of man coming from his limited mind. The prophet is but a mouthpiece of the LORD who says what is spoken to him by the LORD and nothing more, else he is surely a false prophet.

And why is it so important to recognize this fact, to acknowledge clearly the inspiration of Scripture? Because without this faith we lose our closeness to God, we separate ourselves from His presence, which breathes in every word.

The Scroll

Ezekiel took the scroll (as did John) from the hand of the angel and was told to eat it; and so he did. On the scroll were the words of the LORD, the words he was to speak to all, without reservation. The LORD could not make more real the fact that the prophet speaks *His* words (and His words alone). O let us open our mouths faithfully as the prophet!

If only we would consume the Word of God, Holy Scripture; if only it could be the words we speak and the thoughts we think, then perhaps we would have the faith of Ezekiel and John and all who speak for God – then perhaps we would be His children and cease to sow doubt in the Church.

The scroll is so sweet to the taste of those who long for the LORD like a deer for running streams. Though it may become sour in our stomachs, though its speaking may bring us persecution and trial... still they are not deterred who set their souls on serving God. They become His scroll declaring the glory of the LORD to a lost world.

The Finger of the LORD

The words of Holy Scripture are inscribed by the finger of the LORD. This is made abundantly evident with Moses on the mountain receiving the two tablets – which we are specifically told were inscribed by the finger of God – and is just as true for all of the Bible, the Word of God.

The finger of the LORD may be interpreted as the Holy Spirit; and so, all of Scripture is inspired by the Holy Spirit, guided by His Hand... and His Hand is sure, and His Hand is the Hand of God.

The Hand of God is at work here in His Word. This, first of all and most of all, we must always see, we must never lose sight of. This Hand is very real, far more real than the hand of any man, far more powerful than any work of the imagination. It is Truth itself.

And this Word should be inscribed upon our own hearts in a way even more real than on tablets of stone or the pages of a book. We must be the page on which the LORD writes – our hearts must freely accept His Word, yielding to His inspiration like wax to a seal.

O LORD, write your NAME upon our hearts and let our tongues declare your glory.

God Is Present

If we are to be present to God, then we must realize that He is present in His Word. He is present everywhere, it is true, but is especially present in His Word (as in His Sacrament); and if we do not recognize His presence here, we will not recognize His presence anywhere... however much we may tell ourselves otherwise. It will be something other than God to which we will be present: a false god we will own.

And if not present to the LORD, we will not know His love; we will not know love at all. We will call what we conceive "love," but as our god will be false, so will our love. Often becoming quite the opposite of love.

If God is not present to us, we are lost. It is as simple as this. And God comes to us most especially in His Word and in His Sacrament. His Word we must comprehend and profess as His own (and not the work of the imagination of man) or we will be making Him into something other than He is – and we will become an image not of God... for God will not be present in us.

Uphold My Word

The LORD calls all souls to uphold His Word, to declare the Truth of the Scripture He writes for us... But instead those most entrusted with its care serve to undermine His Word, sowing division in its verses and negating its effect, allowing it to be so watered down that it becomes irrelevant. And all because they lack faith.

And so, how can the faith of others be built up; how can it be supported and nourished if the Word itself is diminished in the eyes and ears of those who need its light?

We must uphold the Word of God, set it on a stand as a lamp shining in a dark place, not encourage its being enveloped by darkness itself. O how treacherous is the darkness of doubt to which men surrender their souls blindly! What shall save them from such death?

Only the Word of the LORD can illumine our minds and bring us into His presence. The words of men will inevitably fall short and leave us wanting. And so, let us trust in the Word the LORD provides and we will not bow to specious arguments and have our reason dispossessed but see with the eyes of God the glory shining before us.

No Hope

If we fail to uphold the LORD's Word, there will be no hope, for us or for the world. Christ Himself, who is the Word of God and the Word made flesh, will become of no consequence and the salvation only He brings will be lost – there will only remain condemnation and the terrible violence that comes with it.

The world is in great darkness; as it is, it is condemned. Without the Word of God, indeed it has no hope. And who will uphold His Word if we don't? But will the Lord find any faith on this earth when He returns?

So many things we hold up in place of God and His Word. So many things supplant Him in our hearts and minds. We are principally concerned with the works of our hands, and lose our souls in preoccupation with them. They become our gods and we their slaves, for they rob us of our freedom as children of the LORD.

Our eyes stare into TV screens or other electronic devices... and we become blind to reality, to what is around us, to ourselves... and ultimately to the presence of God, who is most real. We live in an illusory world of our own making. Lost.

Who will uphold the Word of the LORD and its veracity?

The Ember

Let the burning ember be taken from the altar of God and touched to our lips by the angel, that we might stand in the presence of the LORD and declare His glory to all. Our sin must be purged, our hearts made pure, or we shall indeed die at the sight of God.

How our lips need to be purified! It is the tongue that sets the whole body aflame with unholy fire – how polluted our breath and our words become when sin takes possession of our souls! And sin has taken our souls and prevented our knowing the LORD's holy Word.

Your words are sinful, O mortal man. Your thoughts are not like those of YHWH, who speaks in silence the profound truths of the Gospel. Yet you exalt your ways above His and presume the words you speak greater than those of Him who made your tongue. How lost in lies you are!

How we need the ember from the fire before the throne of the LORD to touch us deeply, to reach down to our very spirits and purge us of our pride. For we are sinful people living amongst a sinful people, and so, blind to the presence of our God.

O LORD, let your fire consume our sins that we might stand before you and do your will in all things.

One WORD

The Word of God is one WORD: YHWH. All of Scripture speaks this WORD and comes from this WORD. It is the Breath upon the prophet's soul; he who knows not this WORD is not a prophet. This WORD must speak in every word the prophet utters or his word is worth nothing at all.

The NAME of God must be inscribed upon the heart of the prophet; his spirit must be one with the LORD. If his words come not from this Divine Silence, he knows not of what he speaks, for he speaks not for the LORD but from his own mind and soul. This is not the prophecy of the LORD.

And since so many know not this Silence, since so many are lost in the chatter of the world, they are blind to the inspiration of the Bible, that it is the Word of God. They come to think that God is like them, even as they go further from Him. But He does not change or become polluted – His Word remains sure.

But who will recognize his blindness to the Word of the LORD and humble himself before its glory as a child before its Father? Who will call into question his own mind rather than the Mind of God? And who will continue down a vain road?

The WORD is One; let us bow down to its beauty.

The Still, Small Voice

Do you hear the still, small voice of the LORD speaking in your soul, the whispering sound that frightened Elijah so? He was not disturbed by roaring wind or earthquake or fire, but upon sensing the LORD come so close in His still, small voice, the great prophet retreated to the entrance of the cave on the mountain of God. If you do not hear this voice, if you are not drawn into the presence of the LORD – and frightened thereby – you do not know God or His Word. You are not like His prophet.

This still, small voice is everything, is at the heart of all that Is, for it is the speaking of the NAME of God, who holds all that Is in His hands. He who created all speaks with this still, small voice that pierces the soul of those who listen and penetrates to the marrow of their bones. And though it is wondrous, in the awe it inspires is a deep and reverent fear – how can we know His love without recognizing our falling far short?

The LORD comes close to those whom He loves and chastises them that they might receive the blessing of His presence. Let His still, small voice speak in your soul and you will begin to hear the prophecy of the LORD and come into His dwelling place. (He desires to dwell with you.)

The Sword of the Spirit

The sword of the Spirit pierces the soul, separating soul from spirit and calling us to the heavenly realm. We must leave all behind – whoever loses his life for God's sake will save it.

The Word of the LORD upon the soul of the prophet is like a sword piercing his throat; and the prophet cannot resist its call, cannot fail to speak the words etched upon his heart. It indeed becomes like a burning fire that cannot be contained and cannot be quenched but must be set on a stand for all in the house to see.

And it brings a kind of death to the prophet, cutting him off from his own concerns; much as Elisha boiled his twelve oxen on the yokes he'd used for plowing and gave the meat away, he must be cut off from all of his past life – for whoever puts his hand to the plow and turns back is not fit for the Kingdom of God, and it is to the Kingdom of God and His Word the prophet is called.

His words and thoughts are not his own: the Spirit falls upon him, making him a new man. He bleeds now with Jesus, pierced by the sword of the Spirit, and can only say: "Thus says the LORD," lest he be killed, destroyed by unfaithfulness to his call.

The Lying Spirit

The prophet who speaks with a lying spirit is false: he speaks not the Word of God but seeks to ingratiate himself with his hearer and gain some profit from his words.

Most men are simply foolish, ignorant of the Word of God; having been blinded by their sin, they are unable to understand what God says and so grope in the dark for answers and interpretations. They resort to their own minds, which are patently foolish, lacking sense, and in these they put their trust – knowing not where else to turn.

They indeed sow division in the Word of God by their ignorant words, but there is not the same malice as there is in the lying spirit, in the soul that turns more consciously from the truth in order to advance his cause. This spirit is most unclean and commits the unforgivable sin of confusing truth and lie, thus abandoning the Holy Spirit and the light of salvation He brings.

All things can be forgiven and turned to good by the blood of Christ, but as long as one treasures the lying spirit, his soul will be forever lost. Give yourself over to the LORD and His Word and not to the spirit of the evil one.

Below the Surface

Those without the voice of God speaking in them remain only on the surface of things, and are blind even to what is on the surface; for it is from the depth that is in the heart that even the surface finds its meaning.

And so those deaf to the Word of God offer the most specious arguments, blatantly contradicting themselves and the text of Scripture without even realizing it, for truly those who look only to the surface – or I should say "glance," for there is no sustained look at all – are blind, and worse than blind, for at least the blind know they cannot see and do not attempt to speak of how things appear. But these souls who see not even the skin of things speak with presumed authority and so lead those who listen to them astray. This is a tragedy.

In the LORD alone is found depth and meaning; only in recognition of His voice speaking in Scripture do we begin to see what is written there. We must go below the surface, with faith in the One who moves the speaker, or forever empty will our hearts and minds be – in vanity we shall dwell.

Moses

The foundation for the understanding of prophecy rests upon Moses, to whom the LORD spoke "face to face." Until the coming of Jesus and John's prophecy of His presence, there was no greater prophet than Moses. The Baptist is the greatest of men born of woman because he is the voice crying in the wilderness of the Lamb of God in our midst... but until the arrival of our Savior, Moses stood as the LORD's most blessed servant.

And even Jesus speaks of Moses' composition of the first books of the Bible. Repeatedly He says, "Moses told you..." when addressing the Law come from God. And the Word itself repeatedly assigns Moses as the mediator of the LORD's Word to man.

And so the devil attacks this foundation, knowing that causing it to crumble will cause faith in prophecy and so in God to crumble as well. And so scholars discount Moses as composer of the Pentateuch, preoccupied by all sorts of arbitrary academic exercises that effectively serve to undermine the foundation. They may not know they do the work of Satan, but his work is accomplished all the same. And so the LORD's little ones are led astray, back into the desert of sin. How lost they become!

How shall we rediscover the great power and grace of prophecy, the blessing it is for mortal man? Who will open his ears to the LORD speaking? May Moses pray for the lost souls of modern men.

Elijah

On Mount Carmel Elijah slit the throats of the prophets of Baal, for he had shown that the LORD is God and Baal is not, and that these prophets were leading the people astray.

There is no prophet today who should have his throat slit by anyone's hand – leave any such act to God alone! But how we pray that their lies will be exposed and the people brought back to the Faith by true prophecy, by the Word of God itself. And we pray for those prophets led astray themselves, that they will come to the Truth as well.

Elijah was a great contemplative who lived so much in the wilderness with the LORD alone. He walked forty days to the mountain of God and there heard His silent voice speak piercingly to his soul. He prayed and the rains stopped; he prayed again and they fell – he was a man of powerful prayer. He called down fire from Heaven and was taken aloft in a whirlwind.

And he was hunted down for his faith, for his standing against the lies of the world and the evil powers that be, but he remained strong and proved the fidelity of the LORD and His love for His people.

The LORD is God. With Elijah let us know this to the marrow of our bones (and pray for those who do not know).

John the Baptist

The voice proclaims the Word. The fire upon Elijah falls upon John and he speaks with the power of the Spirit of the Holy

One before his eyes. The Word of God made flesh is in our midst!

This is the great Word of prophecy; this is the culmination of all the prophets and their message to man: Behold the Lamb of God who takes away the sins of the world. He walks among us. Follow Him.

Was there anything of the world that held back the tongue of St. John the Baptist as he cried out in the wilderness of this forsaken earth? Did he restrain himself from declaring the Word of God? Was there some comfort which held sway over his soul or some consideration he gave to the desires of man? Was he a reed moved by the wind?

He was not dictated to by the trends of the time, nor did he seek to appease the powers that be. For this commitment to the Truth he was beheaded... but his voice still speaks in our ears (and in the ears of all who kill the prophets today).

He was not dressed in fine clothes, nor did he receive honors from the world. He was a prophet of God who spoke *His* Word. Who is there desires to be like him?

"I Put My Words into Your Mouth"

As the angel touched the lips of Isaiah with a burning ember from the altar of God, so YHWH Himself extends His hand to Jeremiah and puts His words into the mouth of the prophet, and he cries out the Word of God.

This makes clear as the scroll given Ezekiel and John to eat that it is indeed the LORD's words the prophet speaks. The Word of the LORD burns like a fire in the heart of Jeremiah, and he cannot but speak the words the LORD pours into him. The Spirit pierces to his bones and he must declare the Word of the LORD, or die.

This is the Word of life, the Word that gives life to all whose hearts are open to receive it from the hand of God. For God is life and in His prophecy He shares the life that is His own with every yearning soul. But those who close their hearts and minds and mouths to the life-giving Word spoken by the prophets can but die alone.

These are the words of the LORD, my brother, my sister! The words you hear or read in the pages of the Holy Bible are God's own – they are filled with the Spirit that gives life. Come to them as the prophet, with open mouth and longing heart, and you will live and never die.

"That All Would Be Prophets"

Moses' prayer we see coming to pass in our day. It is most clearly proclaimed by the Second Vatican Council in its declaration of the "universal call to holiness" and witnessed especially in the various movements and orders that have sprung up before and since. This is the age of the laity, for God's Spirit is falling "even upon the menservants and maidservants," as Joel has prophesied (2:29). And so the promises of our Baptism are finally being realized – we so blessed to be Christians are each of us priest, prophet, and king by the grace of our Lord Jesus Christ and in His Name.

The coming to fruition of this sacred call has not been without its problems and confusion – but then Satan never ceases to attack the Church, of course; this, one should never forget. But the work of Satan does not in any way diminish the glorious work of the LORD, which goes forth despite any distraction.

The world becomes ever a darker place, and that darkness affects members of the Church... but the light of the Church grows ever brighter, straining forward toward the Kingdom of God, which becomes more present to us each day in His Word and in His Sacrament, in the heart of all faithful souls.

Eyes to See

Let the prophecy of Isaiah not be fulfilled in us: let us not have ears to hear but hear not, eyes to see but see not. Rather, let our ears and eyes be illumined by faith in God that indeed we might hear His holy Word and see His glory shining before us – that we might come into His living presence.

Why should we be like wood or stone? Why should we follow idols that have no life in them, that indeed make us deaf and blind? Why would anyone be so led astray?

I do not know. But I see it all the time in the commentary of accepted Biblical scholars who so lack faith that they cannot see what is evident before their eyes, even the simplest of things. The devil has somehow led them astray and they have become blind. And remarkably so.

But those who have faith have their eyes opened to see not only the light of the LORD shining in their midst, but also the everyday things of this existence: being thus illumined by the One who illumines the universe, the universe itself becomes comprehensible to their minds. But those without faith not only lose the light of the LORD, they also stumble blindly through this world.

Let us have eyes to see. Let us turn to the LORD and trust in Him (and His Word) alone, and all things will be ours as well.

Presence

In prophecy is the presence of God, and it brings us into the present moment where God dwells. For the LORD is present in His Word and by His Word His presence is made known. By His Word the world was created: He opened His mouth and spoke, and so all that is came to be. And so it is by that Word of the LORD that we come to see who we are and what is all around us, for it is by that Word the LORD Himself is revealed to our mortal eyes. Without His Word we are indeed blind and lost, wandering aimlessly through this world.

God is present, always present – there is never a time or place that He is not. This world is His creation and we are His creation and by His Word all of Creation is kept in existence before His eyes. The question is: are we present with Him? Are we dwelling in His presence, or are we somehow outside His light? If we desire to be in His presence with eyes to see and ears to hear, then we will seek His Word and listen to His Word and act accordingly... and into His presence we will come.

Open your mouth and speak over us your holy Word this day, O LORD, that we might be your children dwelling in your presence by the power of that Word upon us. O let us come into your light!

The Silence within Our Hearts

The Silence of the LORD breathes in our souls and beats in our hearts – His NAME is spoken within us and so we come into His presence. All that matters is that we sit at the feet of Jesus and listen to His voice. If we do not hear Him, we are quite lost.

It is this Silence from which all prophecy comes; the Word of God is rooted in His silent NAME (YHWH). In the presence of God there are no words (for they all fall short of His glory). If we have not this firm foundation, our house will be destroyed when the wind and the rains come. None can stand who do not stand on the Word of God.

O LORD, speak your NAME within us; help us to remember your presence, to be with you at all times and so never lost to the whims of the world. How easily we are distracted! How readily we turn away! Save us, O LORD, from our blindness – let us turn back to you again.

Find the Silence within your heart, my brother, or dare not speak at all. Let your words come from no other place than this solid rock unshakable foundation of faith. Breathe as one with God or your breath will not give life.

Persecution

There is no doubt that the prophet suffers persecution, that he shares in the Cross of Christ, for he speaks the truth and the truth is not something the world wishes to hear... and so it seeks to destroy it.

But the prophet must not fall into anger against his persecutors, sinning as Moses before the stiff-necked complaints of the Israelites in the desert; nor as Jeremiah, whom the LORD exhorted to purify himself of any vile indignation – he must always love his enemy (for this is the greatest prophecy of all).

It is true that only Jesus could do this perfectly, but we must ever strive to follow in His way if the words we speak are to be effective, if our lives are to be worthwhile.

The prophet must expect the persecution and accept the persecution, making excuses for his persecutors like Christ on the Cross, for truly it is out of ignorance that men fight against the enduring Word of God, and truly it is they who suffer most from their persecution.

The prophet, if he is true, will indeed find joy in his sufferings, knowing it is the LORD who is being persecuted and that he is blessed to stand in His stead.

The Potter

The LORD forms us human beings in His own hands, making of us what He pleases (and He has been pleased to make us in His own image). And can He not form His Word, the Scripture He gives us, with His own hands?

Why do Bible commentaries say things like, "The editor attributes this to Moses," when the Word of God clearly states that YHWH spoke to Moses and that Moses wrote down what the LORD said and did what He commanded? Why do they present the prophets as imagining what they think would be best to say? This is blasphemy against the Word of God and reveals a soul tragically blind to the presence of God in His Word and in His prophets. It is they who imagine things and then present them as truth.

Who puts the words into the mouths of these blind prophets? They are not formed by the hand of the LORD, neither the words nor they themselves. And since their words serve to diminish the power of the Word of God, it can only be the evil one for whom they speak, whether consciously or not.

The LORD is the Potter. He is the One who speaks, He is the One who holds all the world in His hands. We must be as clay in His hands, or risk being destroyed.

"Zeal for Your House Consumes Me..."

"... And so I bear the insults they utter against you." As Jesus was, so are His prophets. He is the suffering Servant and they suffer with Him, both before and after His coming in the flesh, because they are indeed possessed of the Word of God that spurs the anger of the reprobate soul.

But the prophet cannot help but speak, cannot cease to be filled with zeal for his LORD and God, despite the death it brings. He is consumed with the love of God, for the love of God has touched him deeply and there is no one who remains unaffected by God's touch. It rivets us in His presence.

Do not fear zeal for the LORD; do not turn from His burning love. It is this alone that will bring you to His Kingdom, that will allow you to participate in the resurrection of the Son. Eternal life is not a facile thing – listen to the Word of the LORD and let it burn in your soul.

It will burn away all evil; it will be a fire consuming all the darkness in your heart and preparing you to enter Heaven. This zeal is a great blessing drawing you into oneness with God.

Truth

O how the truth rings in our souls! O how it pierces our hearts! How undeniable it is to any mind... O how it sets us free!

But to be set free we must be open to the truth; we must welcome it, however painful it might be. The truth cannot be hidden, but people can seek to hide from the truth, even calling for the rocks to fall upon themselves that they might not see the truth.

So many are so afraid of the truth, afraid to face their imperfections, their sins, and their need to repent and reform their lives. They refuse to believe they could be in the wrong, and would do anything to avoid this truth. How hard the heart of man can become.

But how foolish it is to hide from the truth, to fight against it, for, as we have said, the truth cannot be hidden and so will become known; thus any such fight is vain, so vain... and so harmful to our souls.

The prophet may be killed for speaking the truth, but the souls of those who hide from his words will die forever, and this is a much worse fate. For the truth reaches beyond this world and finds its fulfillment in Heaven, where the faithful prophet will be for eternity, but whose way is blocked by a hardened heart.

False Prophecy

How we are surrounded by, immersed in, false prophecy today!

Jeremiah tells Hananiah, who falsely prophecies the end of the Babylonian exile in two years, that the prophet ordinarily speaks of impending war; if he speaks of peace, his words can only be confirmed when they come to pass. And how many speak of peace in their vain promises to the masses – politicians declaring how much good they will do, advertisers promoting the glories of their wares, judges and lawmakers deciding as they please and making up that which will tickle the people's ears...

And in the schools and churches, too, false prophecy prevails, as souls are told that all is well, that it does not matter their sin or their inclination to repent – all are saved: all we do is good and right!

But how different is the mind of Christ, who tells us clearly the gate is narrow and there are few who enter therein; who warns us that the rich man will not come to the Kingdom of Heaven... and exhorts us to take up our cross each day.

To whom do we listen? Are our hearts fooled by the pleasurable sounds of the false prophets of the day; or do we hear the Word of God speaking in our hearts, calling us to die for His sake, and treasure this above all things?

Approaching the LORD

Here I sit (as I have throughout this writing) before the LORD exposed upon the altar. On the ground before the first pew in this chapel, there is nothing between Him and me.

Who could approach the LORD unless He called him? I pray you call me here, dear LORD, and bless all this writing, that I may be a prophet for you, speaking your words, and thus draw souls into your presence.

It is into your presence all hearts long to come, and how blessed is the one who finds himself bathed in your light.

"Emmanuel": the LORD is with us, and we must always be with Him; we must always follow His Word and walk in His way if we are to fulfill our call and dwell with Him forever. His Word is not easy and His way is not broad – to love our enemy He calls all souls, and in this way His love becomes known.

In the end is only silence and the bright shining of light. In the end His Spirit penetrates our senses, filling our eyes and all our bodies with His holy light. In the end love is all that remains. And will we remain with Him? Will we remember His silent NAME and rest in His arms?

In the end nothing exists but what is of the LORD. I pray you remember His presence with you this day.

Printed in the United States
By Bookmasters